For Cats

With Health Problems

By Rupert C. Robertson III

Copyright © 2015 –
Rupert C. Robertson III

* * *

*This book is dedicated to
Ingeborg Hollwoeger,
the ultimate cat lover,
who has spent many a volunteer
hour at our local animal shelter
(The Fairfield Bay Animal Protection
League)
And her constant companions
Pasha and Lilliput*

Table of Contents

Beef and Rice

Beef and Rice

Beef

Beef and Potato

Tuna and Rice

Tuna and Rice

Chicken Liver and Rice

Liver and Rice

Balanced reduced-protein/low-phosphorus

Heart Healthy Recipes

Beef, Rice, Clams, and Chicken Fat Diet

Beef, Clams, and Chicken Fat Diet

Beef, Rice, Clams and Chicken Fat Diet

Beef, Clams and Chicken Fat Diet

Chicken, Rice, Clams and Chicken Fat Diet

Chicken, Clams and Chicken Fat Diet

Tuna, Rice and Clams Diet

Tuna and Clams Diet

Recipe for Cats with Heart Disease

Diets for Cats with Hepatic Disease

Cottage Cheese, Tofu, and Rice Diet (moderate sodium)

Safe, Natural, and Inexpensive Treatment/preventive for Mange, Fleas, and External Parasites*

Can Recipes Be Copyrighted?

Introduction

First, let me state for the record, I am not a veterinarian. I would strongly recommend that you consult with your veterinarian before you adopt a diet program. My only qualifications are that I have done extensive research to try and find out how to help older and ailing dogs and cats.

Over the years, my wife and I have adopted rescue and abandoned dogs and cats. We have watched them struggle with various conditions as they grew older and have searched for ways to prolong their lives without making them suffer. It is difficult, and often very expensive, to find a diet that will help them survive some of the problems associated with aging, kidney, heart and other serious problems.

The recipes that are included in this work are a compilation of the research that we have done to help our own four-legged family members. I hope it is helpful to you. If you mass produce these recipes, you will find that most of them can be done for the same cost (or less) as lower priced canned cat food. They are far less expensive than prescription cat food and better for them, since there are no added preservatives, dyes, flavor enhancers or other unwanted chemicals. This cost does not include labor but, since it is a labor of love, it shouldn't. The reward of seeing your pet healthier is enough to offset the cost of labor.

I have tried to credit all of my sources for these recipes so that you can further research their ideas and credentials. Many are veterinarians and health care professionals, but some are people like you and me that have simply done a lot of research and come up with their own recipe(s). Please, feel free to share any of them with your friends or your local animal shelter. Just give credit when you do. It may help save someone's feline friend.

Kidney

Diets for Management of Chronic Renal Disease in Cats

Recipe for a Cat Food reduced in Protein and Phosphorus

by Natascha Wille

For private use only unless credit is given.

Meat Mix

400 mg Vitamin B Complex
400 IU Vitamin E
4000 mg Taurine
4000 mg Salmon oil
Cod liver oil = 20,000 IU vitamin A
4500 mg Calcium Carbonate
2 raw egg yolks
236 ml (1 cup) cold, distilled water
900 g (2 lbs) ground meat WITHOUT BONE of your choice.
Skinless, if using chicken

Vegetable Mix

450 g (2 cups) canned pumpkin or cooked, pureed squash
or yam

220 g (1 cup) unsalted butter
Yields 14 x 130 g (½ cup) portions.

NOTES:

As suggested in the recipe, use Calcium Carbonate and no other type of Calcium. Calcium Carbonate helps block Phosphorus.

When using canned pumpkin, make sure it is NOT pumpkin pie filling!

Butter is a highly digestible animal fat containing essential fatty acids and naturally occurring vitamins – to add healthy, easily accessible calories for energy. Although butter is derived from milk, it is 81% fat and 18% water. It contains only 0.05% carbohydrates – presumably lactose. Lactose in amounts that minuscule are of no concern.

Preparation:

Combine all supplements from the "Meat Mix" with the distilled water and egg yolk using a whisk. Add meat and combine thoroughly. Set aside.To make the "Vegetable Mix" warm canned pumpkin on low heat in a pot, making sure it does not burn, and melt butter in it. Stir until creamy. Alternatively use fresh squash or yam. Peel, steam-cook, and puree vegetable. Butter can be added will pureeing hot vegetables.Combine Meat Mix with

Vegetable Mix. Make sure that the vegetable mix has cooled to at least body temperature. Stir until an even blend is achieved.

Divide into desired portion sizes, and freeze in favorite containers for storage.

Thanks to http://tcfeline.com/2012/04/27/reduced-protein-cat-food/
Lots of good info here.

Homemade Cat Food

2 medium packs or one Max Pack: Chicken thighs, drumsticks or one whole
chicken (I buy whichever is on sale, but thighs and drumsticks have the most muscle meat, which cats need for the taurine.)

1 large chicken liver container, or 1-2 small containers; or I package of hearts and gizzards
1/2 cup brown rice
2 eggs
Several pats of butter, or a dollop of vegetable oil
(Optional: several dollops of plain yogurt)
1 can peas, or peas and carrots, or 1/2 to one cup of frozen peas, or fresh green
beans, zucchini, carrots (diced)
1 human multi-vitamin (without iron, if possible)
2 human calcium tablets (can also be calcium with magnesium or zinc)
2 human vitamin C tablets
2 fish oil capsules
(Optional: 1 human probiotics tablet)
(Or buy kitty vitamins at the pet store.)
Kitchen shears or pair of scissors

Put chicken in big stew pot with rice, vegetables, and vitamins (except the fish oil.) Add water to cover ingredients, beat eggs, drizzle them into water, add butter, oil or yogurt.

Bring to quick boil, simmer for 45 minutes, then add one of the small containers of chicken livers, or one-quarter or half a large container of livers, or one quarter a pack of hearts and gizzards. Less if you're using muscle meat, more for whole chicken or white meat.

Add the fish oil capsules.

Simmer for another 15 minutes or so.

Let mixture cool, and then pick the chicken off the bones, discard the bones, and cut meat, skin, liver, or hearts and gizzards into small pieces (easiest with kitchen shears or scissors.)

Return meat to pot and stir into the liquid and vegetables mix. Scoop out and freeze portions (I save the containers from the chicken livers and freeze the cat food in them, or you can use ziplock bags.)

Should feed a medium-size cat for two weeks, or more.

Simmer leftover chicken livers separately, and whenever your cat is finicky about the new food, sprinkle some liver on top and he'll scarf it right down (too much liver isn't good for them, so do it sparingly.) Or add a little tuna to their bowl to encourage them to the new food. (You can also throw a can of tuna into your large chicken recipe, or any other fish, canned clams -- occasionally.)

Freeze any leftover liver (or gizzards and hearts) and add to your next batch of cat food.

I let one container or bag thaw at a time, refrigerate it, and feed Felix from that. It has more nutrition than canned or dried food, so you may not need to put out as much at one time in their bowl. When Felix is done, if there's any left in his bowl, I refrigerate that, and bring it out for the next meal.

(This recipe can also be made with fish --not highly salted-- with canned clams for the taurine; beef or hamburger with beef liver and/or kidneys. But chicken probably comes closest to a wild diet.)

You might want to cut open the fish oil capsules, in case they don't dissolve easily on their own.

Exact measurements aren't necessary, and you can vary any of the recipes slightly, because it doesn't matter if the cat gets exactly the same level of nutrients in each and every meal.

http://www.dailykos.com/story/2012/03/11/1073417/-HEALTHIER-CATS-w-HOME-MADE-CAT-FOOD#

Yield: About 6 cups; provides about 5-6 days food.

1 and 1/3 cups (2/3 lb. ground chicken, turkey or lean heart)

4 cups Well-cooked soft, basmati rice (add an additional 1/2 cup of water to the recipe and cook it longer, this will make it easier to digest).

4 eggs

2 tablespoons of a good cold-pressed oil, (can be alternated with unsalted butter)

1 teaspoon finely chopped parsley, finely grated carrot (optional)

1/8 teaspoon iodized sea salt

1/8 teaspoon potassium chloride salt substitute

1,500 mg calcium

5,000 IU vitamin A

50 mg level vitamin B complex (the equivalent of about 10 mg/day)

2,500 mg vitamin C (1/2 teaspoon sodium ascorbate)

Cat vitamins with taurine (about 5 days worth)

Mix all ingredients together (except the

vitamins/supplements) in a large bowl. Bake in a moderate oven for about 20 minutes. Allow to cool, then add the vitamins and mix well. (If you cat has a poor appetite you may have to experiment to some extent to cater to his/her preferences just to keep him nourished). Store in fridge. If you warm your cats food before you serve it DO NOT use the microwave to do it. Instead put the food in a small glass dish in a hot water bath to warm it. Microwaves change the molecular structure of protein. It will also ruin the vitamins.

Variation: Occasionally include a small amount of calf, beef or chicken liver in the recipe (1-3 teaspoons).

http://petremedycharts.blogspot.com/2011/01/kidney-diets-for-older-cats.html

petremedy RECIPE #2

4 parts carbohydrate: Pureed barley flakes and /or baby food creamed corn

2 parts protein: Lightly broiled chicken or beef or raw organic egg yolk and cooked white (used with meat, not alone) you can also use baby food chicken

1 part vegetable: Chopped of finely grated raw vegetable or vegetable juice-carrots, zucchini, and alfalfa sprouts are best

2 Tablespoons of a powdered feline vitamin and mineral supplement

2 teaspoons soft butter

Blend above ingredients together and store in glass jar.

Each day mix the following into each meal:

A feline vitamin and mineral supplement (follow label instruction)

1/16 teaspoon ascorbic acid crystals or sodium ascorbate powder (250 units Vitamin C)

1/8 teaspoon Pet Tinic (a B vitamin and iron tonic available from the veterinarian) or 1/2 of a low-potency B complex capsule (10 mg level)

1/4 teaspoon or 1/2 tablet mixed digestive enzymes.

Once a week give:

400 units of vitamin E (alpha tocopherol);

A capsule containing 10,000 units vitamin A and 400 units vitamin D.

http://petremedycharts.blogspot.com/2011/01/kidney-diets-for-older-cats.html

White meat chicken, chicken gizzard plus 2 hard-boiled eggs with a touch of clam juice or chicken broth: 20%
Kidney beans, mashed: 10%
Well-cooked white/basmati rice (I add an additional 1/2 cup of water or vegetable broth to the rice cooking instructions and cook it longer. It makes the rice much softer and easy to digest, polenta, barley: 60 %
Parsley, squash, asparagus, carrot kale: 10%

http://petremedycharts.blogspot.com/2011/01/kidney-diets-for-older-cats.html

petremedy RECIPE #4

Feline Restricted Mineral and Sodium Diet

1 lb. Regular ground beef, cooked
1/4 lb. Liver (beef, chicken or pork only), cooked
1 cup cooked enriched white rice without salt
1 teaspoon vegetable oil
1 t (5 grams) calcium carbonate
1/8 teaspoon KCl (salt substitute)

Also add a balanced supplement which fulfills the feline
MDR for all vitamins and trace minerals, and 250 mg
taurine/day.

http://petremedycharts.blogspot.com/2011/01/kidney-
diets-for-older-cats.html

Chicken Mineral Broth

The recipe below is not a specific for renal disease but it is very nourishing and helpful to have on hand if your cat looses interest in food and doesn't want to eat. Nutritionally it can help replace minerals that have been lost if your cat is urinating excessively.

3 lbs. chicken thighs
Water to cover Distilled water is my preference
1/4 cup tomato juice (NOT, V8 Juice)
Add approximately 1 1/2 inch piece of Kombu, (this is a dried sea vegetable) for added minerals

Put all chicken into a soup pot large enough so the chicken fills the pot only halfway. Cover with 'distilled' water until water is one to two inches above chicken. Cover the pot loosely (tip the lid). Bring to a low simmer. Simmer three to five hours, occasionally breaking up the chicken and adding more water if necessary. During the last hour remove the lid and let the water cool down until the chicken is barely covered. Broth is now deliciously strong. Pour off broth, cool to room temperature, and then store in refrigerator.

Pour this broth off and store it with the first batch of broth. Transfer the bones into a smaller pot. Crack them up so they form a fairly compact mass in the bottom of the pan. Cover the bones with water ad add the one-fourth cup tomato juice. Simmer one-half to one hour.

Pour off this broth, again combining it with the other broth. Throw the bones away. Store about two cups of the broth in a jar in the refrigerator; store the rest in the freezer in pint-sized covered freezer containers to be thawed as needed. To thaw, stand the container in a bowl of hot water.

http://petremedycharts.blogspot.com/2011/01/kidney-diets-for-older-cats.html

Recipe one can be made up in advance and provides enough food for one cat for around 6 days. It boasts a high percentage of usable protein while having low phosphorus and sodium levels. The recipe also has great levels of vitamin B complex along with vitamin A.

Ingredients you will need are as follows:

- 1 cup of ground chicken or turkey
- 4 cups of cooked basmati rice – adding an extra ½ cup of water will ensure the rice is extra well cooked and therefore easier for your cat to digest
- 4 eggs
- 2 tbs of good quality cold-pressed olive oil
- 1 tsp of finely chopped parsley
- 1/8th tsp of iodised sea salt
- 1/8th tsp of potassium chloride salt substitute

Vitamins and Supplements to be added to the mix include the following:

- 1,500 mg of calcium
- 5,000 IU vitamin A
- 50 mg vitamin B complex
- 2,500 mg vitamin C

- Taurine cat vitamin supplements – 5 days worth

Preparation

Mix the first lot of ingredients together in a large bowl before baking the mix in a moderate oven for around 20 minutes or so. Next, you need to allow the mixture to cool before adding in all the vitamins and supplements making sure they are well mixed in. Place the mixture in a container and store this in the fridge. To warm the food up before feeding a portion to your cat, place a bowl of food in a larger bowl filled with hot water and leave for a couple of minutes.

Note: If your cat is a fussy eater, you may need to play around with the ingredients to find out which they like best. You should never change a cat's diet suddenly because it could upset their stomachs. It is far better to do this gradually over a couple of weeks or so.

http://www.pets4homes.co.uk/pet-advice/2-homemade-recipes-for-cats-suffering-from-kidney-disorders.html

For Cats on a Restricted Mineral and Sodium Diet

This is a great recipe for cats that need to be put on a restricted mineral and sodium diet. It's simple to prepare and very easy to add all the necessary supplements which cats need included in their diet. The following recipe makes enough to last one cat 4 to 5 days.

Ingredients you will need are as follows:

1 lb cooked minced meat - beef
1/4lb cooked liver – preferably chicken, beef or pork
1 cup cooked white rice very well cooked
1 tsp vegetable oil 5 grams calcium carbonate 1/8 teaspoon of a salt substitute

A cat specific supplement that contains all the vitamins and trace minerals as well as taurine (250 mg per day) – this needs to be mixed in the food on a daily basis

Preparation

Place all the meat and vegetable oil in a pan and simmer until fully cooked. You need to then overcook the rice by adding extra water to the pot, this makes it easier for cats to digest. Let both the meat and the rice cool down before mixing together while adding in the salt substitute and the calcium carbonate making sure it is well mixed in.

Next, divide the mix into four or five portions and place in containers in the fridge ready to be fed to your cat. You need to add the cat specific supplement to the mix each day, making sure it's well mixed in with the meat and rice.

http://www.pets4homes.co.uk/pet-advice/2-homemade-recipes-for-cats-suffering-from-kidney-disorders.html

Chicken and Rice

Low Protein, Low phosphorus, Normal Potassium, Normal Sodium
Diet Providing 55 Grams Protein/1000 Kcalorie Diet

1/4 cup cooked chicken breast (72 grams)
1/2 ounce clams, canned, chopped in juice (14 grams)
1/2 cups cooked rice, white polished, long-grain (80 grams)
1 tablespoons chicken fat (14grams)
1/8 teaspoon salt substitute-potassium chloride
1 calcium carbonate tablets (400 mg calcium)
1/4 multiple vitamin-mineral tablet
1/10 tablet B complex vitamin-trace mineral

provides 297 kcalories, 16.3 g protein, 14.5 g fat
See table for caloric needs of cats
provides phosphorus 48%, potassium 215%, sodium 169% of a cat's daily needs
To feed this diet with a normal amount of phosphorus substitute 2 grams bone meal powder for the 1 calcium carbonate tablet

http://dogcathomeprepareddiet.com/diet_and_chronic_renal_disease.html

Chicken and Rice

Low Protein, Low phosphorus, Normal Potassium, Normal Sodium
Diet Providing 46.4 Grams Protein/1000 Kcalorie Diet

1/4 cup cooked chicken breast (72 grams)
1/2 ounce clams, canned, chopped in juice (14 grams)
1 cups cooked rice, white polished, long-grain (160 grams)
1 tablespoons chicken fat (14 grams)
1/8 teaspoon salt substitute-potassium chloride
1 calcium carbonate tablets (400 mg calcium)
1/4 multiple vitamin-mineral tablet
1/10 tablet B complex vitamin-trace mineral

provides 399 kcalories, 18.5 g protein, 14.7 g fat
See table for caloric needs of cats
provides phosphorus 43%, potassium 164%, sodium 124% of a cat's daily needs.
To feed this diet with a normal amount of phosphorus substitute 2 grams bone meal powder for the 1 calcium carbonate tablet.

http://dogcathomeprepareddiet.com/diet_and_chronic_renal_disease.html

Egg White and Rice

Protein, Low phosphorus, Normal Potassium, Normal Sodium
Diet Providing 53 Grams Protein/1000 Kcalorie Diet

3 whites from whole chicken eggs, cooked
2 ounce clams, canned, chopped in juice (57 grams)
1 cups cooked rice, white polished, long-grain (160 grams)
1 tablespoons chicken fat (14 grams)
1/8 teaspoon salt substitute-potassium chloride
1 ½ calcium carbonate tablet (600 mg calcium)
1/4 multiple vitamin-mineral tablet
1/10 tablet B complex vitamin-trace mineral

provides 312 kcalories, 19.7 g protein, 13.8 g fat
See table for caloric needs of cats
provides phosphorus 41%, potassium 341%, sodium 603% of a cat's daily needs.
To feed this diet with a normal amount of phosphorus substitute 2 grams bone meal powder for the 1 1/2 calcium carbonate tablets

http://dogcathomepreppareddiet.com/diet_and_chronic_renal_disease.html

Egg White and Rice

Low Protein, Low phosphorus, Normal Potassium, Normal Sodium
Diet Providing 46.6 Grams Protein/1000 Kcalorie Diet

2 whites from whole chicken eggs, cooked
2 ounce clams, canned, chopped in juice (57 grams)
1 cups cooked rice, white polished, long-grain (160grams)
1 tablespoons chicken fat (14 grams)
1/8 teaspoon salt substitute-potassium chloride
1 1/2 calcium carbonate tablet (600 mg calcium)
1/4 multiple vitamin-mineral tablet
1/10 tablet B complex vitamin-trace mineral

provides 399 kcalories, 18.6 g protein, 13.9 g fat
See table for caloric needs of cats
provides phosphorus 41%, potassium 341%, sodium 603% of a cat's daily needs.
To feed this diet with a normal amount of phosphorus substitute 2 grams bone meal powder for the 1 1/2 calcium carbonate tablets

http://dogcathomepbrepareddiet.com/diet_and_chronic_renal_disease.html

Eggs

Low Protein, Low phosphorus, Normal Potassium, Normal Sodium
Diet Providing 54.2 Grams Protein/1000 Kcalorie Diet

2 cooked whole eggs, chicken
1/2 ounce clams canned, chopped in juice (14 grams)
1 tablespoon chicken fat (14 grams)
1/8 teaspoon salt substitute-potassium chloride
1 calcium carbonate tablet (400 mg calcium)
1/4 multiple vitamin-mineral tablet
1/10 tablet B complex vitamin-trace mineral

provides 308 kcalories, 16.7 g protein, 25 g fat
See table for caloric needs of cats
provides phosphorus 89%, potassium 274%, sodium 673% of a cat's daily needs.
Bone meal need not be used in this diet to increase phosphorus content.

http://dogcathomepreparedDiet.com/diet_and_chronic_renal_disease.html

Eggs and Rice

Low Protein, Low phosphorus, Normal Potassium, Normal Sodium
Diet Providing 45.7 Grams Protein/1000 Kcalorie Diet

2 cooked whole eggs, chicken
1/2 ounce clams canned, chopped in juice (14 grams)
1/2 cups cooked rice, white polished, long-grain (80 grams)
1 tablespoon chicken fat (14 grams)
1/8 teaspoon salt substitute-potassium chloride
1 calcium carbonate tablet (400 mg calcium)
1/4 multiple vitamin-mineral tablet
1/10 tablet B complex vitamin-trace mineral

provides 411 kcalories, 18.8 g protein, 25.2 g fat
See table for caloric needs of cats
provides phosphorus 69%, potassium 189%, sodium 440% of a cat's daily needs.
To feed this diet with a normal amount of phosphorus substitute 1 grams bone meal powder added to 1/2 calcium carbonate tablet

http://dogcathomeprepareddiet.com/diet_and_chronic_renal_disease.html

Chicken and Potato

Low Protein, Low phosphorus, Normal Potassium, Normal Sodium
Diet Providing 57.4 Grams Protein/1000 Kcalorie Diet

1/2 cup cooked chicken breast (142 grams)
1/2 ounce clams canned, chopped in juice (14 grams)
1/2 cup potatoes boiled in skin (62 grams)
2 tablespoons chicken fat (28 grams)
1 1/2 calcium carbonate tablets (600 mg calcium)
1/4 multiple vitamin-mineral tablet
1/10 tablet B complex vitamin-trace mineral

provides 453 kcalories, 26 g protein, 30.6 g fat
See table for caloric needs of cats
provides phosphorus 52%, potassium 198%, sodium 201% of a cat's daily needs.
To feed this diet with a normal amount of phosphorus substitute 2 grams bone meal powder for the 1 1/2 calcium carbonate tablets

http://dogcathomeprepareddiet.com/diet_and_chronic_renal_disease.html

Chicken and Potato

Low Protein, Low phosphorus, Normal Potassium, Normal Sodium
Diet Providing 46.2 Grams Protein/1000 Kcalorie Diet

1/3 cup cooked chicken breast (95 grams)
1/2 ounce clams canned, chopped in juice (14 grams)
1/2 cup potatoes boiled in skin (62 grams)
2 tablespoons chicken fat (28 grams)
1 1/2 calcium carbonate tablets (600 mg calcium)
1/4 multiple vitamin-mineral tablet
1/10 tablet B complex vitamin-trace mineral

provides 418 kcalories, 19.3 g protein, 29.9 g fat
See table for caloric needs of cats
provides phosphorus 47%, potassium 198%, sodium 172% of a cat's daily needs.
To feed this diet with a normal amount of phosphorus substitute 2 grams bone meal powder for the 1 1/2 calcium carbonate tablets

http://dogcathomeprepareddiet.com/diet_and_chronic_renal_disease.html

Beef and Rice

Low Protein, Low phosphorus, Normal Potassium, Normal Sodium
Diet Providing 56.8 Grams Protein/1000 Kcalorie Diet

4 ounces (raw weight) lean ground beef, cooked (114 grams)
1/2 ounce clams canned, chopped in juice (14 grams)
1/2 cups cooked rice, white polished, long-grain (80 grams)
1 tablespoon chicken fat (14 grams)
1 1/2 calcium carbonate tablets (600 mg)
1/4 multiple vitamin-mineral tablet
1/10 tablet B complex vitamin-trace mineral

provides 443 kcalories, 25.2 g protein, 26.6 g fat
See table for caloric needs of cats
provides phosphorus 52%, potassium 123%, sodium 206% of a cat's daily needs.
To feed this diet with a normal amount of phosphorus substitute 2 grams bone meal powder for the 1 1/2 calcium carbonate tablets

http://dogcathomeprepareddiet.com/diet_and_chronic_renal_disease.html

Beef and Rice

Low Protein, Low phosphorus, Normal Potassium, Normal Sodium
Diet Providing 44.3 Grams Protein/1000 Kcalorie Diet

4 ounces (raw weight) lean ground beef, cooked (114 grams)
1/2 ounce clams canned, chopped in juice (14grams)
1/2 cups cooked rice, white polished, long-grain (80 grams)
2 tablespoon chicken fat (28 grams)
1 1/2 calcium carbonate tablets (600 mg)
1/4 multiple vitamin-mineral tablet
1/10 tablet B complex vitamin-trace mineral

provides 569 kcalories, 25.2 g protein, 40.5 g fat
See table for caloric needs of cats
provides phosphorus 45%, potassium 105%, sodium 175% of a cat's daily needs.
To feed this diet with a normal amount of phosphorus substitute bone 2 grams meal powder for the 1 1/2 calcium carbonate tablets.
Add 1/8 teaspoon potassium chloride to increase potassium content.

http://dogcathomeprepareddiet.com/diet_and_chronic_renal_disease.html

Beef

Low Protein, Low phosphorus, Normal Potassium, Normal Sodium
Diet Providing 55.3 Grams Protein/1000 Kcalorie Diet

4 ounces (raw weight) lean ground beef, cooked (114 grams)
1/2 ounce clams canned, chopped in juice (14 grams)
5 teaspoons chicken fat (24 grams)
1 calcium carbonate tablets (400 mg calcium)
1/4 multiple vitamin-mineral tablet
1/10 tablet B complex vitamin-trace mineral

provides 430 kcalories, 23.8 g protein, 35.8 g fat
See table for caloric needs of cats
provides phosphorus 50%, potassium 126%, sodium 234% of a cat's daily needs.
To feed this diet with a normal amount of phosphorus substitute 2 grams bone meal powder for the 1 calcium carbonate tablets.
Add 1/8 teaspoon potassium chloride to increase potassium content.

http://dogcathomepreepareddiet.com/diet_and_chronic_renal_disease.html

Beef and Potato

Low Protein, Low phosphorus, Normal Potassium, Normal Sodium
Diet Providing 46.7 Grams Protein/1000 Kcalorie Diet

4 ounces (raw weight) lean ground beef, cooked (114 grams)
1/2 ounce clams canned, chopped in juice (14 grams)
1/2 cup potatoes boiled in skin (62 grams)
2 tablespoons chicken fat (28 grams)
1 1/2 calcium carbonate tablets (400 mg calcium)
1/4 multiple vitamin-mineral tablet
1/10 tablet B complex vitamin-trace mineral

provides 540 kcalories, 25.2 g protein, 40.5 g fat
See table for caloric needs of cats
provides phosphorus 46%, potassium 194%, sodium 185% of a cat's daily needs.
To feed this diet with a normal amount of phosphorus substitute 2 grams bone meal powder for the 1 1/2 calcium carbonate tablets.

http://dogcathomeprepareddiet.com/diet_and_chronic_renal_disease.html

Tuna and Rice

Low Protein, Low phosphorus, Normal Potassium, High Sodium
Diet Providing 53.4 Grams Protein/1000 Kcalorie Diet

3 ounces tuna, canned in water (86 grams)
1/2 ounce clams canned, chopped in juice (14 grams)
1/2 cups cooked rice, white polished, long-grain (80 grams)
2 tablespoons chicken fat (28 grams)
1/8 teaspoon salt substitute-potassium chloride
1 1/2 calcium carbonate tablets (600 mg calcium)
1/4 multiple vitamin-mineral tablet
1/10 tablet B complex vitamin-trace mineral

provides 468 kcalories, 25 g protein, 30 g fat
See table for caloric needs of cats
provides phosphorus 50%, potassium 190% of a cat's daily needs, sodium depends on using low salt tuna.
To feed this diet with a normal amount of phosphorus substitute 2 grams bone meal powder for the 1 1/2 calcium carbonate tablets

http://dogcathomeprepareddiet.com/diet_and_chronic_renal_disease.html

Tuna and Rice

Low Protein, Low phosphorus, Normal Potassium, High Sodium
Diet Providing 44.8 Grams Protein/1000 Kcalorie Diet

2 ounces tuna, canned in water (57 grams)
1/2 ounce clams canned, chopped in juice (14 grams)
1/3 cups cooked rice, white polished, long-grain (53 grams)
2 tablespoons chicken fat (28 grams)
1/8 teaspoon salt substitute-potassium chloride
1 calcium carbonate tablets (400 mg calcium)
1/4 multiple vitamin-mineral tablet
1/10 tablet B complex vitamin-trace mineral

provides 406 kcalories, 18.2 g protein, 29.6 g fat

http://dogcathomeprepareddiet.com/diet_and_chronic_renal_disease.html

Chicken Liver and Rice

This comes from Small Animal Clinical Nutrition, 4th Edition (a veterinary nutrition textbook).
For a 4.5g (10lb) cat you can use the following recipe for daily amounts.

Cooked chicken liver--21g
Cooked white rice (may substitute rice baby cereal and flavor with meat broth during cooking)--98g
Cooked white chicken--21g
Vegetable oil--7g
Calcium carbonate--0.7g
Iodized salt--0.5g
Salt substitute (KCl)--0.5g
1/2 human multivitamin
1 to 1/2 taurine tablet (500mg/tablet)

Liver and Rice

1/4 cup chopped liver

1/8 cup rice

1/8 cup pumpkin

1/2 chopped egg

1 teaspoon of yogurt

From a friend at the local animal shelter

Balanced reduced-protein/low-phosphorus

Daily food formulation for a 4.5-kg cat (as fed)

Ingredients	Grams
Liver, chicken cooked	21
Rice, white cooked	98
Chicken, white cooked	21
Oil, vegetable	7
Calcium carbonate	0.7
Salt, iodized0.5Salt, substitute (KCl	0.5
Total	149

Nutrient Content (%DMB)+

Dry matter	37.8
Protein	24.4
Fat	17.5
Linoleic acid	7.9
Crude Fiber	0.85
Calcium	0.54
Phosphorus	0.29
Magnesium	0.09
Sodium	0.42
Potassium	**0.66
Energy(kcal/100g)	458*

Also feed one-half tablet to cats to ensure all vitamins and trace minerals are included. Cats should be given one-half to one taurine tablet (500mg/tablet) daily. May substitute rice baby cereal and flavor either selection with meat broth during cooking. *Retain the fat. †Nutrients of concern are italicized.

Directions: Cook the meat components separately until well done. Cook the starch component. Grind or finely chop meat if necessary. Mix with all other components except the vitamin-mineral supplement. Mix well and serve immediately or cover and refrigerate. Feed the vitamin-mineral supplement with the meal; give as a pill or pulverize and thoroughly mix with food before feeding.

Read more at: https://tr.im/U2N1C Thanks to: http://www.petplace.com/

Heart Healthy Recipes

Beef, Rice, Clams, and Chicken Fat Diet
(Normal protein, normal potassium, minimum sodium)

8 ounces lean ground beef (raw weight), cooked
1/2 cup rice, long-grain, cooked
1 ounce clams, chopped in juice
1/2 tablespoon chicken fat
2 bonemeal tablets (10-grain or equivalent) or 1/2
teaspoon bonemeal powder
1/2 calcium carbonate tablet (200 milligrams calcium)
1 multiple vitamin-mineral tablet

Provides 590 kilocalories, 48.7 grams protein, 31.6 grams
fat
Consult with your veterinarian to determine how much to
feed!
Provides potassium at 164 percent, sodium at 276 percent,
magnesium at 167 percent of a cat's daily needs

http://bigheartsfund.org

Beef, Clams, and Chicken Fat Diet
(Normal protein, normal potassium, moderate sodium)

8 ounces lean ground beef (raw weight), cooked
1 ounce clams, chopped in juice
1/2 tablespoon chicken fat
1 bonemeal tablet (10-grain or equivalent) – OR- 1/4 teaspoon bonemeal powder
1 calcium carbonate tablet (400 milligrams calcium)
1 multiple vitamin-mineral tablet

Provides 487 kilocalories, 46.6 grams protein, 31.4 grams fat
Consult with your veterinarian to determine how much to feed!
Provides potassium at 202 percent, sodium at 362 percent, magnesium at 174 percent of a cat's daily needs
http://bigheartsfund.org

Beef, Rice, Clams and Chicken Fat Diet
Normal Protein, Normal Potassium, Minimum Sodium

8 ounces (raw weight) lean ground beef, cooked (228 grams)
1/2 cup cooked rice, white polished, long-grain (80 grams)
1 ounce clams, chopped in juice (28.5 grams)
1/2 tablespoon chicken fat (7 grams)
1/4 teaspoon bone meal powder (1.5 grams)
1/2 calcium carbonate tablet (calcium 200 mg)
1 multiple vitamin mineral tablet

590 kcalories, 48.7 g protein, 31.6 g fat
Use table on cat caloric requirements to determine how much to feed
provides potassium 164 percent, sodium 276 percent, magnesium 167 percent of cat's daily needs

http://www.dogcathomepreppareddiet.com

Beef, Clams and Chicken Fat Diet
Normal Protein, Normal Potassium, Moderate Sodium

8 ounces (raw weight) lean ground beef, cooked (228 grams)
1 ounce clams, chopped in juice (28.5 grams)
1/2 tablespoon chicken fat (7 grams)
1/4- teaspoon bone meal powder (1 grams)
1 calcium carbonate tablet (calcim 400 mg)
1 multiple vitamin mineral tablet

provides 487 kcalories, 46.6 g protein, 31.4 g fat
Use table on cat caloric requirements to determine how much to feed
provides potassium 202 percent, sodium 362 percent, magnesium 174 percentof cat's daily needs

http://www.dogcathomeprepareddiet.com

Chicken, Rice, Clams and Chicken Fat Diet
Normal Protein, Normal Potassium, Moderate Sodium

1 cup cooked chicken breast (285 grams)
1/2 cup cooked rice, white polished, long-grain (80 grams)
1 ounce clams, chopped in juice (28.5 grams)
1 tablespoon chicken fat (14 grams)
1/4- teaspoon bone meal powder (1 grams)
1 calcium carbonate tablet (calcium 400 mg)
1 multiple vitamin mineral tablet

provides 475 kcalories, 50.2 g protein, 18.1 g fat
Use table on cat caloric requirements to determine how much to feed
provides potassium 150 percent, sodium 308 percent magnesium 203 percent of cat's daily needs

http://www.dogcathomeprepareddiet.com

Chicken, Clams and Chicken Fat Diet
Normal Protein, Normal Potassium, Moderate Sodium

1 cup cooked chicken breast (285 grams)
1 ounce clams, chopped in juice (28.5 grams)
1 tablespoon chicken fat(14grams)
1/4- teaspoon bone meal powder (1 grams)
1 calcium carbonate tablet (calcium 400 mg)
1 multiple vitamin mineral tablet

provides 372 kcalories, 48.1 g protein, 17.9 g fat
Use table on cat caloric requirements to determine how much to feed
provides potassium 189 percent, sodium 409 percent, magnesium 232 percentof cat's daily needs

http://www.dogcathomeprepareddiet.com

Tuna, Rice and Clams Diet
Normal Protein, Normal Potassium, Minimum Sodium

5 1/2 ounces tuna, canned in water (low sodium) (157 grams)
1 ounce clams, chopped in juice (28.5 grams)
1/2 cup cooked rice, white polished, long-grain (80 grams)
1 tablespoon chicken fat (14 grams)
1/4- teaspoon bone meal powder (1 grams)
1 calcium carbonate tablet (calcium 400 mg)
1 multiple vitamin mineral tablet

provides 431 kcalories, 46.4 g protein, 16.6 g fat
Use table on cat caloric requirements to determine how much to feed
provides potassium 149 percent, sodium low depending on content in tuna fish, magnesium 605 percent of cat's daily needs

http://www.dogcathomeprepareddiet.com

Tuna and Clams Diet

Normal Protein, Normal Potassium, Minimum Sodium

5 1/2 ounces tuna, canned in water (low sodium) (157 grams)
1 ounce clams, chopped in juice (28.5 grams)
1 tablespoon chicken fat (14 grams)
1 calcium carbonate tablet (calcium 400 mg)
1 multiple vitamin mineral tablet

provides 328 kcalories, 44.3 g protein, 16.4 g fat
Use table on cat caloric requirements to determine how much to feed
provides potassium 200 percent, sodium low depending on content in tuna fish, magnesium 808 percent of cat's daily needs

http://www.dogcathomeprepareddiet.com

Recipe for Cats with Heart Disease

Balanced low-sodium/low-mineral homemade formulas for adult cats with heart disease*:

Daily food formulation for a 4.5-kg cat (as fed)

Ingredients	Grams
Beef, lean cooked	67
Rice, white, cooked*	67
Calcium carbonate	0.7
Salt, iodized0.1Salt, substitute (KCl	0.1

Total135	Nutrient Content (%DMB)+
Dry matter	37.9
Protein	36.4
Fat	21.5
Linoleic acid	0.73
Fiber	0.65
Calcium	0.55
Phosphorus	0.28
Magnesium	0.07
Sodium	0.17
Potassium	0.54
Energy (kcal/100g)	500

*Also feed one-half tablet to cats to ensure all vitamins and trace minerals are included. Cats should be given one-half to one taurine tablet (500mg/tablet) daily.

Retain the fat.

*May substitute rice baby cereal and flavor either selection with meat broth during cooking.

†Nutrients of concern are italicized.

Directions: Cook the meat component until well done. Cook the starch component separately. Grind or finely chop meat if necessary. Mix with all other components except the vitamin-mineral supplement and taurine. Mix well and serve immediately or cover and refrigerate. Feed the vitamin-mineral supplement and taurine with the meal; give as a pill or pulverize and thoroughly mix with food before feeding.

http://www.petplace.com/ Read more at: https://tr.im/COtuz

Diets for Cats with Hepatic Disease

Cottage Cheese, Tofu, and Rice Diet (moderate sodium)

1/3 cups white rice, cooked (53 grams)
1/2 cup cottage cheese, 1% fat (113 grams)
2/3 cup tofu, raw firm (169 grams)
1 ounce clams, chopped in juice (29 grams)
1 tablespoon chicken fat (14 grams)
1/4- teaspoon bone meal powder (1 grams)
 1/4 multiple vitamin tablet for humans

provides 466 calories, 40.9 g protein, 22.6 g fat, .416% sodium
a 10 pound cat needs 318 calories per day (286 calories for 9 pound and 350 calories for 11 pound cat)
One to 2 ounces or more of raw potato (23 kcalories/ounce) can be used to increase bowel movement frequency

dogcathomeprepareddiet.com/

Tofu and Rice Diet (low sodium)

1/3 cups white rice, cooked (53 grams)
1 cup tofu, raw firm (252 grams)
1 ounce clams, chopped in juice (29 grams)
1 tablespoon chicken fat (14 grams)
1/4- teaspoon bone meal powder (1 grams)
 1/4 multiple vitamin tablet for humans

provides 463 calories, 36.3 g protein, 25 g fat, .036% sodium
a 10 pound cat needs 318 calories per day (286 calories for 9 pound and 350 calories for 11 pound cat)

dogcathomeprepareddiet.com/

Turkey and Rice Diet (low to moderate sodium)

1/3 cups white rice, cooked (53 grams)
1/3 pound (raw weight) turkey, cooked (152 grams)
1/4- teaspoon bone meal powder (1 grams)
1/4 multiple vitamin tablet for humans

provides 321 calories, 28.3 g protein, 15.4 g fat, .133% sodium
a 10 pound cat needs 318 calories per day (286 calories for 9 pound and 350 calories for 11 pound cat)
One to 2 ounces or more of raw potato (23 kcalories/ounce)
can be used to increase bowel movement frequency
dogcathomepreparreddiet.com/

Cat Diarrhea

1/2 cup rice, long-grain, boiled
1 cup boiled chicken breast, chopped into bite sized pieces

Instructions: Mix together two ingredients, and add a small amount of the chicken broth to help mix the ingredients.

Adding fibre: Pumpkin either boiled or canned (not the pie filler variety, which contains sugar) can also be added to the diet. This can help to bulk up the food.

From Cat World

Recipe 2 for cat with diarrhea:

1/2 cup rice, long-grain, boiled
1 cup beef mince, boiled

Instructions:
Mix together two ingredients and add a small amount of the beef broth to help mix the ingredients.

Adding fibre: Pumpkin either boiled or canned (not the pie filler variety, which contains sugar) can also be added to the diet. This can help to bulk up the food.

From Cat World

Obese Cats

Recipe for Overweight Cats

Daily food formulation for a 4.5-kg cat (as fed)

Ingredients	Grams
Liver, chicken, cooked	125
Rice, white, cooked	46
Cereal, All Bran	8
Calcium carbonate	1.2
Salt, iodized0.3Salt, substitute (KCl)	0.3
Total	180

Nutrient Content	(%DMB)
*Dry matter	33.8
Protein	52.7
Fat	11.4
Linoleic acid	1.2
Fiber	5.2
Calcium	0.85
Phosphorus	0.77
Magnesium	0.11
Sodium	0.44
Potassium	0.67
Energy (kcal/100g)	420

*Also feed one one-half tablet to cats to ensure all vitamins and trace minerals are included. Cats should be given one-half to one taurine tablet (500mg/tablet) daily.

May substitute rice baby cereal and flavor either selection with meat broth during cooking.

*Nutrients of concern are italicized.

Directions: Cook the meat component well . Cook the starch component separately. Grind or finely chop meat if necessary. Mix with all other components except the vitamin-mineral supplement. Mix well and serve immediately or cover and refrigerate. Feed the vitamin-mineral supplement with the meal; give as a pill or pulverize and thoroughly mix with food before feeding.

http://www.petplace.com/ Read more at: https://tr.im/KHYBi

General Cat Food Recipes

Kitty Heaven

Ingredients:
2 flat cans of sardines packed in oil
1 tsp liver
2/3 cup cooked rice
1/4 cup parsley, chopped

Instructions:
Combine all ingredients. Stir with wooden spoon to break up sardines into bite size pieces. Store unused portions in refrigerator, tightly covered.

Thanks to Maumelle Friends of the Animals, Jo Garrison

Here Kitty, Kitty Dinner

Ingredients:
1 cup boiled chicken
¼ cup shredded carrots, steamed
¼ cup fresh broccoli, steamed
¼ cup chicken broth

Instructions:
Combine all ingredients with chicken broth so that it holds together. This same recipe can be used with fish that is broiled until it flakes. You may also vary the recipe by adding rice or other vegetables.

Thanks to Maumelle Friends of the Animals, Jo Garrison

Vitamin Rich Meal For Cats

Ingredients:
½ cup small curd cottage cheese
1 tsp. chopped liver
1 pinch of iodized salt
2 tbsps Bisquick
1 tsp corn oil

Instructions:
Thoroughly combine all ingredients. Store unused portions
in refrigerator, tightly covered.

Thanks to Maumelle Friends of the Animals, Jo Garrison

Homemade Cat Food For Everyday
The Cat-Lover's Cookbook, Tony Larson

Ingredients:
½ pound, filet of sole
2 tbsp parsley, chopped
water
¼ cup grated cheddar cheese
½ tsp iodized salt
2 tbsp onion, chopped
Salt and pepper
1 tbsp butter
½ cup milk
2 tbsp chopped liver
2/3 cup cooked egg noodles, chopped small (or 2/3 cup cooked rice)

Instructions:
          Put sole in a small greased baking dish. Sprinkle with onion, parsley and a dash of salt and pepper. Add enough water to cover just the bottom of the dish. Cook in a pre-heated, 450 degree, oven for 10 minutes. Remove from oven, cool and cut into kitty size pieces. Melt butter in small sauce pan. Stir in flour and heat until bubbling. Gradually stir in the milk and cook, stirring constantly until mixture thickens. Add cheese, liver and salt, stirring until cheese has melted. DO NOT BOIL. Add chopped fish and noodles to cheese sauce and stir well. Cool and serve.

Yields 4 to 6 servings. Store unused portions in an airtight container and keep refrigerated.

Cat Treats

Jo-Jo's Mackerel Cat Munchies

Ingredients:
1/2 cup canned mackerel, drained
1 tsp corn oil
1/2 tsp. brewers yeast
1 cup whole grain bread crumbs
1 egg, beaten

Instructions:
Preheat oven to 350 degrees. In a medium sized bowl, mash the mackerel with a fork until it is in tiny pieces. Combine it with the remaining ingredients and mix well. Drop mixture by 1/4 teaspoons onto a greased cookie sheet. Bake for 8 minutes. Cool to room temperature and store in an airtight container in the refrigerator.

Thanks to Maumelle Friends of the Animals, Jo Garrison

Tuna/Salmon Fudge

Ingredients:
2 – 6 oz cans of tuna **or** 1 - 14 oz can of salmon (do not drain)
1 tbsp garlic powder or minced garlic
1 tbsp grated parmesan cheese
1-1/2 cups flour
2 eggs

Instructions:
Preheat oven to 350 degrees. Process fish, garlic and eggs in food processor or blender. Add flour and mix to a brownie-like consistency. Spread into a 9 X 9 inch greased pan and bake for 20 minutes. When brownies are done, they will have a putty-like texture and the edges will pull away from the pan. Cut into squares and freeze.

Thanks to Maumelle Friends of the Animals, Lynne and Bryna

Hairball Control

Most of the sites I have researched recommend grain-free cat foods for hairball control. They can prevent hairballs because they are easier on your cat's digestion. That means find foods with no wheat, gluten, barley, rice, corn. Other types of solutions/help mentioned are natural products that will help to naturally lubricate and coat the stomach, aiding in the animals ability to pass the excess hair rather than allowing it to build up.

For instance:

Add some canned pumpkin or bran to each of your cat's meals (about a spoonful)

Place a small amount of non-petroleum jelly on the nose of your cat so that the animal can lick it off. Make sure it is non-petroleum.

About once a week, add a teaspoon of fish oil to your cat's food.

Also very important: Groom your cat often during shedding season

Natural Hairball Remedy Recipe

From: Herbalogue's Species-Appropriate Natural Hairball Remedy Recipe for Cats

This recipe is primarily for hairball control and also works to condition their skin and coat while promoting organ and joint health as well as cognitive function. It is loaded with vitamins and minerals the cats actually use and need to maintain good health.

The exact recipe is:

1 Raw egg, yolk only (organic, cage free, brown egg is best to use for avoiding foreign hormones and antibiotics from being passed on to your pet)

Cod liver oil 30g / ~1 oz. (plain, unflavored, no additives, etc. There is a brand by Nordic Naturals named Pet Cod Liver Oil specifically for cats and dogs.)

Combine the yolk and cod liver oil together until it is evenly mixed.

The dose given to a healthy adult cat should be approximately 1/8 - 1/4 teaspoon total product with a meal or afterwards. Depending on the frequency of hairball problems, at the lower end of measurement, it can be given daily (and also find out what the real root of the problem is!) The supplement should be refrigerated, stored out of the light for up to 10 days and offered at room temperature. (Gently shake or turn your product to re-combine before serving if there is any separation.)

Worms

Natural Cat Wormer Treats

1 large or 2 small cans of any flavor wet cat food*
¼ cup of olive oil, canola oil, or coconut oil
1 cup of cooked rice
1 small container of PLAIN unflavored yogurt
½ cup of unsweetened applesauce or pure pumpkin
1 cup of food grade diatomaceous earth (DE)**

Slowly mix all ingredients together, being careful not to inhale the DE or get it in your eyes; it is not toxic but can irritate mucous tissues. It the mixture appears too dry, add small amounts of oil, water, and/or pumpkin until it is very thick but sticks together well. Roll mixture into small balls. Keep a few in a closed container in the refrigerator to give to your cat, and freeze the rest for future use.

If your cat does not have a weight problem, you may feed these treats as often as you want to. If your cat is plump, limit the treats to one a day. This will keep your cat free of most parasites and is safer than prescription meds because it is non-toxic, and you cannot overdose with it.

*never substitute cat for dog food, as their nutritional and protein needs are different

**Use ONLY food grade DE (available at most farm supply stores or online). Check the outside package to ensure that you are getting food grade, which is safe for animals and humans. The DE used in swimming pools contains additives that are toxic to animals.

Thanks to AGTL

Remedys

Put one cup of food grade diatomaceous earth in an old sock, and tie it securely. Take your pet outside, and rub the sock over its body, being careful to avoid the eye area. The DE will seep through the sock fabric and onto the hair. Massage the DE down to the skin. Use regularly, as needed, for a natural preventive or mild infestation. If your cat grooms regularly and licks some of the DE from its hair, there is no problem**

*If your pet has a severe infestation that does not respond to DE treatment, see a veterinarian.

**Ingesting small amounts of DE is beneficial to animals and humans and has a variety of health benefits.

Thanks to AGTL

Can Recipes Be Copyrighted?

I included this section so that you can read about the legalities of sharing these recipes. I encourage you to share them with anyone who has a four legged family member who is suffering and is in need of dietary help. You may reduce suffering and extend the life of someone's beloved pet.

Via Kottke, a <u>Washington Post article on protection of recipes</u>

One should distinguish between a recipe, a textual rendering of a recipe, and a compilation of recipes. Publications Intl. v. Meredith, 88 F.3d 473 (7th Cir. 1996) dealt with alleged infringement of a recipe book:

"The identification of ingredients necessary for the preparation of each dish is a statement of facts. There is no expressive element in each listing; in other words, the author who wrote down the ingredients for "Curried Turkey and Peanut Salad" was not giving literary expression to his individual creative labors. Instead, he was writing down an idea, namely, the ingredients necessary to the preparation of a particular dish. "[N]o author may copyright facts or ideas. The copyright is limited to those aspects of the work—termed 'expression'— that display the stamp of the author's originality." Harper & Row, 471 U.S. at 547, 105 S.Ct. at 2223. We do not view the functional listing of ingredients as original within the meaning of the Copyright Act.

Nor does Meredith's compilation copyright in DISCOVER DANNON extend to facts contained within that compilation. As the Supreme Court stated in Feist: Facts, whether alone or as part of a compilation, are not original and therefore may not be copyrighted. A factual compilation is eligible for copyright if it features an original selection or arrangement of facts, but the copyright is limited to the particular selection or arrangement. In no event may copyrights extend to the facts themselves. Feist, 499 U.S. at 350-51, 111 S.Ct. at 1290. The lists of ingredients lack the requisite element of originality and are without the scope of copyright. The Copyright Office itself has stated that "mere listing[s] of ingredients or contents" are not copyrightable. 37 C.F.R. s 202.1. The next question is whether the directions for combining these ingredients may warrant copyright protection.

The DISCOVER DANNON recipes' directions for preparing the assorted dishes fall squarely within the class of subject matter specifically excluded from copyright protection by 17 U.S.C. s 102(b). Webster's defines a recipe as: a set of instructions for making something ... a formula for cooking or preparing something to be eaten or drunk: a list of ingredients and a statement of the procedure to be followed in making an item of food or drink ... a method of procedure for doing or attaining something. WEBSTER'S THIRD NEW INTERNATIONAL DICTIONARY (Merriam-Webster 1986). The recipes at issue here describe a procedure by which the reader may produce many dishes featuring Dannon yogurt. As such, they are excluded from copyright protection as either a "procedure, process, [or] system." 17 U.S.C. s 102(b).

Meredith fashioned processes for producing appetizers, salads, entrees, and desserts. Although the inventions of "Swiss 'n' Cheddar Cheeseballs" and "Mediterranean Meatball Salad" were at some time original, there can be no monopoly in the copyright sense in the ideas for producing certain foodstuffs.

Nor can there be copyright in the method one might use in preparing and combining the necessary ingredients. Protection for ideas or processes is the purview of patent. The order and manner in which Meredith presents the recipes are part and parcel of the copyright in the compilation, but that is as far as it goes. As Professor Nimmer states: This conclusion [i.e., that recipes are copyrightable] seems doubtful because the content of recipes are clearly dictated by functional considerations, and therefore may be said to lack the required element of originality, even though the combination of ingredients contained in the recipes may be original in a noncopyright sense. 1 MELVILLE B. NIMMER & DAVID NIMMER, NIMMER ON COPYRIGHT s 2.18[I], at 2- 204.25-.26 (May 1996)."

Made in the USA
Lexington, KY
07 June 2018